Rough Guides

25 Ultimate experiences

Italy

Make the most of your time on Earth

ROUGH GUIDES

25 YEARS 1982–2007

NEW YORK • LONDON • DELHI

Contents

Introduction

EXPERIENCES have always been at the heart of the Rough Guide concept. A group of us began writing the books **25 years ago** (hence this celebratory mini series) and wanted to share the kind of travels we had been doing ourselves. It seems bizarre to recall that in the early 1980s, travel was very much a minority pursuit. Sure, there was a lot of tourism around, and that was reflected in the guidebooks in print, which traipsed around the established sights with scarcely a backward look at the local population and their life. We wanted to change all that: to put a country or a city's popular culture centre stage, to highlight the clubs where you could hear local music, drink with people you hadn't come on holiday with, watch the local football, join in with the festivals. And of course we wanted to push travel a bit further, inspire readers with the confidence and knowledge to break away from established routes, to find pleasure and excitement in remote islands, or desert routes, or mountain treks, or in street culture.

Twenty-five years on, that thinking seems pretty obvious: we all want to experience something real about a destination, and to seek out travel's **ultimate experiences**. Which is exactly where these **25 books** come in. They are not in any sense a new series of guidebooks. We're happy with the series that we already have in print. Instead, the **25s** are a collection of ideas, enthusiasms and inspirations: a selection of the very best things to see or do – and not just before you die, but now. Each selection is gold dust. That's the brief to our writers: there is no room here for the average, no space fillers. Pick any one of our selections and you will enrich your travelling life.

But first of all, take the time to browse. Grab a half dozen of these books and let the ideas percolate ... and then begin making your plans.

Mark Ellingham
Founder & Series Editor, Rough Guides

25

Ultimate
experiences
Italy

Spotting Giotto in Padua

t could be argued that the frescoes in Padua's **Cappella degli Scrovegni** are the single most significant sequence of paintings in all of Italy. The masterpiece of Giotto, these pictures mark the point at which the spirit of humanism began to subvert the stylized, icon-like conventions of medieval art – Giotto's figures are living, breathing people who inhabit a three-dimensional world, and for many subsequent artists, such as Masaccio and Michelangelo, the study of Giotto was fundamental to their work. But in addition to being of supreme importance, the frescoes are immensely fragile, having been infiltrated by damp rising from the swampy ground on which the chapel is built, and by moisture exhaled by millions of admiring tourists. Extraordinary measures have been taken to save the chapel from further damage: only 25

visitors at a time are allowed in, for just a quarter of an hour, and entrance is via an elaborate air-lock.

The chapel was commissioned in 1303 by Enrico Scrovegni in atonement for the usury of his father, who died screaming "give me the keys to my strong box" and was denied a Christian burial. As soon as the walls were built, Giotto was commissioned to cover every inch of the interior with illustrations of the lives of Jesus, Mary and Joachim (Mary's father), and the story of the Passion, arranged in three tightly knit tiers and painted against a backdrop of saturated blue. There's little precedent in Western art for the psychological tension of these scenes – the exchange of glances between the two shepherds in *The Arrival of Joachim* is particularly powerful, as are the tender gestures of *Joachim and Anna at the Golden Gate* and *The Visit of Mary to Elizabeth*. And look out for what's said to be Giotto's self-portrait in the fresco of the *Last Judgement* – he's among the redeemed, fourth from the left at the bottom.

need to know

In winter there's a fair chance that you won't have to wait for long before getting into the chapel, but the only way to be certain is to reserve a ticket, either by phoning ℡049.201.0020 at least 48 hours ahead (Mon–Fri 9am–7pm, Sat 9am–1pm), or by booking online at ⓦwww.cappelladegliscrovegni.it at least 24 hours ahead.

The Apennines stretch for eight hundred miles down the very spine of Italy. They are Italy at its roughest and least showy. But these mountains are far from dull. In their loftiest and most rugged stretch, in the central region of Abruzzo, two hours from Rome, you'll find peaks rising up from gentle pastures, and swathes of beech woodland that roll up from deep valleys before petering out just short of the steepest ridges. Such is the landscape of the **Parco Nazionale d'Abruzzo**. Romans come here to walk, climb and enjoy rustic foods like wild boar prosciutto and local sheep's cheese, washed down by the hearty Montepulciano d'Abruzzo wine. Foreign visitors are rare, and you can walk for hours without seeing another person.

This tranquillity isn't lost on the park's wildlife. Chamois, roe deer, martens and even wolves have found a haven here, and the park is also one of the last refuges in Western Europe of the Marsican brown bear. They haven't survived by being easy to spot. After the furtive lynx – an animal which stalks its prey by night before launching an attack that can only be described as explosive – bears are among the park's most elusive creatures. You may be lucky enough to see one briefly, tantalizingly exposed while crossing an exposed mountain ridge. You're more likely, however, to find just paw prints or rocks overturned in the hunt for moths.

The best base is Pescasseroli, a ridge-top village with a cluster of homely hotels and a park visitor centre. From here, you can hike straight into the forest and up along the long ridge that crests and falls from Monte Petroso (2247m) to the aptly named Monte Tranquillo (1830m) and on to Monte Cornacchia (2003m). Or you can take a bicycle on hundreds of kilometres of rough roads that thread through the area. By the time you've done this, you will have earned your plate of wild boar.

need to know

Pescasseroli lies on the single paved road that runs through the heart of the park, and is fairly well served by buses. An excellent walkers' hotel, the *Albergo Al Castello*, 1 Via d'Annunzio, Pescasseroli (℡ & ℻0863.910.757), has simple rooms and does inexpensive meals.

Bears and Boars
Trekking in the
Abruzzo National Park

2

One of the greatest art experiences in Italy is also one of its best-kept secrets. And for that you have to thank not the Italians, but the French, whose embassy has occupied Rome's **Palazzo Farnese** for the past century or so. Inside, Anibale Carracci's remarkable ceiling fresco, the *Loves of the Gods*, was until relatively recently almost entirely off-limits, open only to scholars, VIPs, and those with a proven interest in Renaissance art. Now, with a little planning, it's possible to see it for yourself, and it's perhaps one of the most extraordinary pieces of work you'll see in Rome apart from the Sistine Chapel; plus you get to view it with a small group of art lovers rather than a huge scrum of other tourists.

The work was commissioned from the then unknown Bolognese painter, Annibale Carracci, by Odoardo Farnese at the turn of the sixteenth century to decorate one of the rooms of the palace. It's a work of magnificent vitality, and seems almost impossible that it could be the work of just one man. In fact, it wasn't. Annibale devised the scheme and did the main ceiling, but the rest was finished by his brother and cousin, Agostino and Lodovico, and assistants like Guido Reni and Guercino, who went on to become some of the most sought-after artists of the seventeenth century. The central painting, with its complex and dramatically arranged figures, great swathes of naked flesh, and vivid colours, is often seen as the first great work of the Baroque era, a fantastic, fleshy spectacle of virtuoso technique – and perfect anatomy. The main painting, centring on the marriage of Bacchus and Ariadne, which is supposed to represent the binding of the Aldobrandini and Farnese families, leaps out of its frame in an erotic hotchpotch of cavorting, surrounded by similarly fervent works illustrating various classical themes. Between and below them, nude figures peer out – amazing exercises in perspective that almost seem to be alongside you in the room. Carracci was paid a pittance for the work, and died a penniless drunk shortly after finishing it, but the triumph of its design, and the amazing technical accomplishment of its painting, shines brighter than ever.

need to know There are tours of the **Palazzo Farnese** every Monday and Thursday at 3pm, 4pm and 5pm. You must book in advance, either by email to ©visitefarnese@france-italia.it, or by going to the consular office at Via Giulia 251 (℗06.6889.2818). Admission is free you but must take your passport or some other form of ID with you.

3

Sharing the Loves of the Gods

at the Palazzo Farnese

4 Hiking

An exhilarating sense of triumph overtakes you as you climb the crest of a jagged, snow-laced limestone peak. From your roost above the valley floor, Cortina's campanile and the hotel where you had breakfast this morning are barely visible. The most spectacular climbing routes in the Dolomites are now within your grasp. You've suddenly joined the ranks of the world's elite alpine climbers— or so you would like to think. Actually, most of the credit goes to the cleverly-placed system of cables, ladders, rungs and bridges known as Via Ferrata, or "Iron Way."

the Via Ferrata

These fixed-protection climbing paths were first created by alpine guides to give clients access to more challenging routes. During World War I, existing routes were extended and used to aid troop movements and secure high mountain positions. But today, hundreds of Via Ferrata routes enable enthusiasts to climb steep rock faces, traverse narrow ledges and cross gaping chasms that would otherwise be accessible only to experienced rock jocks.

With the protective hardware already cemented into the rock, you can climb most Via Ferrata routes without a rope, climbing shoes or the rack of expensive hardware used by traditional rock climbers. With just a helmet, harness and clipping system, you fix your karabiner into the fixed cable, find your feet on one of the iron rungs and start climbing. It's an amazingly fun way to conquer some stunning vertical terrain and quickly ascend to airy alpine paths.

Via Ferrata climbing doesn't require polished technique, exceptional strength, balance or even prior rock climbing experience. It does demand decent aerobic conditioning for a sustained ascent of several hundred vertical meters. Once you put aside any fear of heights, you'll find a secure and surefooted excitement in this aerial playground.

need to know
The Dolomites are home to about 300 Via Ferrata routes. The greatest availability of routes is centered around Cortina d'Ampezzo in the eastern Dolomites. Local shops cater to independent climbers with maps and equipment rental. The Gruppo Guide Alpine (www.guidecortina.com) offers a wide range of guided day trips; or you can stay at scenic mountain huts and go from one route to another. The season runs from late June to mid-September, with August bringing the fairest weather but busiest climbs.

5

Getting the
measure of the
Medicis

It's a simple equation: Florence was the centre of the Italian Renaissance; the Medici were the greatest art patrons of Renaissance Florence; their collection was bequeathed to the city by the last Medici, Anna Maria Lodovica; therefore the **Uffizi Gallery** – which occupies offices (*uffizi*) built for the Medici in 1560 – is the greatest display of Renaissance painting in the world. Which is why the Uffizi attracts more visitors than any other building in Italy – more than one and a half million of them every year.

The key to enjoying the Uffizi is to book your ticket in advance and to ration yourself: if you try to see everything you'll barely be able to skate over the surface. For your first visit, limit yourself to the first eighteen rooms or so – this will take you as far as the Bronzino portraits in the octagonal Tribuna. Arranged more or less chronologically, the Uffizi encapsulates the genesis of the Renaissance in a room of three altarpieces of the *Maestà* (Madonna Enthroned) by Duccio, Cimabue and Giotto. After a diversion through the exquisite late-Gothic art of Simone Martini and Gentile da Fabriano the narrative of the Renaissance resumes with Paolo Uccello's *The Battle of San Romano* and continues with Piero della Francesca, Filippo Lippi (and his son Filippino), and of course Botticelli: it doesn't matter how many times you've seen photos of them, the *Primavera* and the *Birth of Venus* will stop you in your tracks. And there's still Leonardo da Vinci to come before you reach the halfway point.

Should you decide to make a dash to the end you'll see a remarkable collection of Venetian painting (Giorgione, Giovanni Bellini, Paolo Veronese, Tintoretto and no fewer than nine Titians), a clutch of fabulous Mantegnas and Raphaels, and the extraordinary *Doni Tondo*, the only easel painting Michelangelo ever came close to completing. Ahead of you are fabulous pieces by Dürer, Holbein and Cranach, del Sarto and Parmigianino, Caravaggio and Rembrandt, Goya and Chardin. Wherever you stop in the Uffizi, there's a masterpiece staring you in the face.

need to know

The Uffizi is open Tues–Sun 8.15am–6.50pm; in high summer and at festive periods it sometimes stays open until 10pm. Ticket reservations can be made at Door 3, or on the Firenze Musei line – ☎055.294.883. Latest details on ⓦwww.firenzemusei.it.

The capital of the Italian South, Naples is quite unlike anywhere else in Italy. It's a city of extremes, fiercely Catholic, its streets punctuated by bright neon Madonnas cut into niches and its miraculous cults regulating the lives of people here almost much as they always did. None more so than the cult of San Gennaro, Naples' patron saint, whose dried blood, kept in a vial in the cathedral, spontaneously liquefies three times a year, thereby ensuring the city's safety for the months to come. It is supposed to take place on the first Saturday in May, on 19 September – San Gennaro's feast day – and also on 16 December, and the liquefaction (or otherwise) of San Gennaro's blood is the biggest annual event in the city's calendar by far, attended by the great and the good of the city, not to mention a huge press corps.

The blood is supposed to liquefy during a mass, which you can attend if you get to the Duomo early enough (ie the middle of the night). The doors open at 9am, when a huge crowd will have gathered, and you're ushered into the church by armed *carabinieri*, who then stand guard at the high altar while the services goes on, the priest placing the vial containing the saint's blood on a stand and occasionally taking it down to see if anything has happened, while the faithful, led by a group of devout women called the "*parenti di San Gennaro*", chant prayers for deliverance. The longer it takes, the worse the portents for the city are. And if it doesn't liquefy at all… well, you will know all about it. It didn't happen in 1944, the last time Vesuvius erupted, and in 1980, when a huge earthquake struck the city, so people are understandably jumpy. Luckily, the blood has been behaving itself for the past couple of decades, a period which has coincided to some extent with the city's resurgence. As the mayor of Naples commented the last time it liquefied: "it's a sign that San Gennaro is still protecting our city, a strong sign of hope and an encouragement for everyone to work for the common good". You may not believe in any of it, of course, but being here while it is all going on is an experience like no other.

need to know

The **Duomo** is on Via Duomo, close to the end of Via dei Tribunali, one of the main streets of Naples' old centre, and ten minutes' walk from the city's main train station.

Going with the Flow in Naples: the Miracle of San Gennaro

6

Enjoying Da Vinci's
Last Supper

It was always busy, and boisterous crowds still line up around the Santa Maria delle Grazie convent in Milan, sometimes for hours in the summer. But these days viewing Leonardo Da Vinci's *Last Supper* has been imbued with a renewed sense of wonder, mystery and above all, conspiracy. Worn, heavily thumbed copies of Dan Brown's bestseller give some indication of what's on their minds: does the image of John really look like a woman? Is there a triangle (the symbol for "holy grail") between Jesus and John? Put such burning questions aside for a moment, and use your precious fifteen minutes to focus on the real wonder inside - Da Vinci's exquisite artistry.

need to know Visits must be booked by telephone at least two or three weeks in advance (reservations on ☎02.8942.1146, Mon–Fri 9am–7pm). It's open Tues–Sun 8am–7.30pm; €6.50 plus €1.50 booking fee). You get 15 minutes inside.

The Renaissance master was in his forties when he painted his depiction of Christ and the twelve disciples, a mural that also served as an experiment with oil paints, a decision that led to its decay in Da Vinci's own lifetime. A shadow of its former self, the epic 21-year restoration, completed in 1999, has nevertheless revealed some of the original colours, and Da Vinci's skills as a painter: his technique is flawless, the painting loaded with meaning and symbolism. Light draws attention to Jesus who sits at the centre, having just informed his disciples that one of them will betray him. The genius of the painting is the realism with which Da Vinci shows the reaction of each: Andrew on the left, his hands held up in utter disbelief; Judas, half in shadow, clutching his bag of silver; Peter next to him, full of rage; and James the Greater on the right, his hands thrown into the air.

Housed in the sealed and climate-controlled refectory of the convent, the focus on just one great work, combined with the laborious process of booking a slot and lining up to get in (25 at a time) heightens the sense of expectation. Once inside there's usually a dramatic change in atmosphere - viewers become subdued, often overwhelmed by the majesty of the painting, and just for a second they stop looking for that elusive grail.

Falling in love with Capri came quickly and easily. I was living in Rome, and some friends had a historic family villa in the heart of the island. Going down for long weekends soon became a regular ritual.

The enigma of the place is that there are really two Capris: the stunning, magical island gulped down all in one mad dash by day-trippers; and the unassuming, yet more captivating Capri, privy, only to those who decide to spend the night.

Day visits mean barely enough time to hike up to Villa Jovis or over to the Arco Naturale, to wander a bit through the chic shops of Capri town and have bite to eat, to take the harrowing bus-ride up to Anacapri and from there the chairlift up to Monte Solaro. Trying to fit in the Blue Grotto requires foregoing at least one of the other major attractions. The experience is satisfying enough but it means never getting away from the crowds.

A stay, however, means savouring the glow of dusk on the sea, with the distant lights of Naples twinkling under the Milky Way, later sipping *limoncello* in a restaurant where Capri resident Graham Greene might have dined. Then rising early to see the sun come up over the Bay of Naples, perhaps from atop a sheer cliff, at which point you will understand why everyone from Roman emperors to writers have found solace and inspiration here – even Lenin reportedly said that "Capri makes you forget everything." Maybe what he really meant was that it makes you remember yourself. Get to know it even a little, and Capri can feel like your true, timeless home. Take your time to seek out the breathtaking lookout points, the secret grottoes and silent groves and you will find a serene world that's yours, and yours alone.

8
Finding yourself on Capri

need to know
Reaching Capri is easy
– take one of the plentiful
hydrofoils from Naples or
ferries from Sorrento. For the
most bucolic stay, choose
accommodation away from
Capri town. On the way up
to **Villa Jovis**, **Villa Sarah**
offers relaxation and views,
while in Anacapri, **Villa
Eva** and **Da Gelsomina
Migliera** are wonderful
guesthouses; @www.
caprionline.com has more
information.

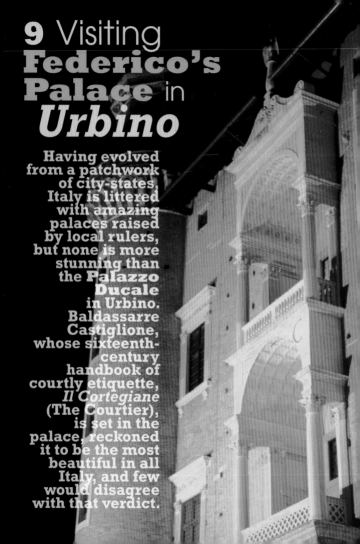

9 Visiting Federico's Palace in *Urbino*

Having evolved from a patchwork of city-states, Italy is littered with amazing palaces raised by local rulers, but none is more stunning than the **Palazzo Ducale** in Urbino. Baldassarre Castiglione, whose sixteenth-century handbook of courtly etiquette, *Il Cortegiane* (The Courtier), is set in the palace, reckoned it to be the most beautiful in all Italy, and few would disagree with that verdict.

Dominating this attractive little university town in the heart of the rural province of Marche, the **Palazzo Ducale** was commissioned in 1468 by **Federico da Montefeltro**, one of the most remarkable men of his era. A brilliant soldier, Federico kept the coffers of **Urbino** full by selling his military services but he was also a man of genuine learning and a great patron of the arts. A friend of the great architect and theorist **Leon Battista Alberti**, he regarded architecture as the highest form of aesthetic activity, and studied the subject so throughly that it was written of him that "no lord or gentleman of his own day knew as much about it as he did." His residence – designed primarily by the otherwise obscure **Luciano Laurana** – is unforgettable testimony to his discernment.

From the street it's not an especially handsome building, but once you step into the **Cortile d'Onore** you'll see what this place is all about: elegant, exquisitely crafted yet unostentatious, it's the perfect blend of practicality and discrete grandeur. Inside, many of the rooms are occupied by the **Galleria Nazionale delle Marche**, where one of the prize exhibits is a portrait of Federico by **Pedro Berruguete** – he's painted, as always, in profile, having lost his right eye in battle. In Federico's private suite of rooms you'll see paintings by the finest of all the artists he sponsored, **Piero della Francesca**, including the enigmatic *Flagellation*. Two adjoining chapels – one dedicated to Apollo and the Muses, the other to the Christian God – are indicative of the complexity of the duke's world-view, as is the astounding **Studiolo**, where wall panels of inlaid wood create some startling illusory perspectives – you'll see some delicately hued landscapes of Urbino here, and portraits of great men ranging from Homer and Petrarch to Solomon and St Ambrose.

need to know
The Palazzo Ducale is open Mon 8.30am–2pm, Tues–Sun 8.30am–7.15pm; €8.

Bologna has more nicknames than Sean Combs. It's "La Dotta" or "The Learned", for its ages-old university, one of the first in Europe; "La Rossa" or "The Red", for the color of its politics. But its most deserving nickname is "La Grassa" or "The Fat" for the richness of its food. After all, even fiercely proud fellow Italians will acknowledge, when pressed, that Bologna's cooking is the best in the country.

This gourmet-leaning university city doesn't expect starving students to shell out a month's rent for a fine meal, either. It's the last major Italian centre where lunch with wine barely breaks 10 a head, and 25 will buy a de luxe, multi-course dinner. The only people who should shun are vegetarians and calorie counters: dishes here are meaty and diet-busting – the Bolognese traditionally chow down on cured hams, game and creamy pasta sauces. Smells of smoked meat waft onto the sidewalk from the old-fashioned grocery-cum-canteen, *Tamburini*, off the main square; it's staffed with old, white-uniformed men, brandishing hocks of ready-to-slice prosciutto amid a clatter of dishes at lunchtime as dozens of locals jostle around the dining room. The via delle Pescherie Vecchie nearby is still jammed with traditional market stalls, fallen produce squishing on the street and sharp-voiced women heckling the stall holders over prices.

But Bologna's love of food is clearest through its drinks: specifically, at cocktail hour, when in bars you can load up for free on *stuzzichini*, Italy's hefty answer to tapas, for as long as you nurse that G&T. With its cream sofas, sparkly chandelier and thirty-something crowd, the *Café de Paris* serves a buffet of watermelon slices and tortilla wraps; while the minimalist *Nu Lounge* nearby, on the colonnaded gallery known as the Buca San Petronio, has fancier nibbles, like dates wrapped in ham or martini glasses full of fresh chopped steak tartare.

need to know

Tamburini, via Caprarie 1, ☎051.234.726, ⓦwww.tamburini.bo.it
Café de Paris, piazza del Francia 1, ☎051.234.980
Nu Lounge, via de'Musei 6, ☎051.222.532, ⓦwww.nulounge.com

10

Chewing the Fat

A Glutton's Tour of
Bologna

SIMONI
Il Famoso Salame
di Felino (Parma)
€17,90 al kg
Metà o Intero

Treading where once only royals and aristos held sway is an everyday occurrence in Italy: once-forbidding palaces, castles and gardens are now open to all. One of the most exhilarating former royal enclaves is a celebration of the sheer wonder of nature, the Parco del Gran Paradiso – a pristine alpine wilderness that lies within yodelling distance of the Swiss Alps and Mont Blanc.

King Vittorio Emanuele II donated what had been the private hunting grounds of the House of Savoy to the Italian state in 1922. The rapacious royals had managed to see off the entire population of bears and wolves, but the scimitar-horned ibex – now the majestic symbol of the park – and the park's other native mountain goat species, the chamois, survived, and now thrive in the protected environment. Even the golden eagle has been reintroduced, and currently numbers about ten pairs, while the other animals of size that you may encounter are cuddly-looking marmots, which, along with perky martens, are the preferred quarry of the major birds of prey.

In winter, the park is paradise indeed for skiers, particularly those of the cross-country variety, from its base in the enticing village of Cogne. However most visitors come to the park in the warmer months, when the rocky heights are spectacularly pure and the hundreds of species of vibrant wildflowers dazzle the eye – and when you're also more likely to spot wildlife. The verdant valley slopes and vertiginous ridges are all traversable by kilometres of walking and hiking trails of all degrees of difficulty, which in turn link any number of refuges where you can spend the night. There's climbing, too, throughout all of the ten valleys. You could try an assault on the 4000-metre-high summit of Gran Paradiso itself – a not particularly difficult ascent if you have the right equipment, and guides – or the more gentle trek up to the sanctuary of San Besso, a two-hour hike to over 2000 metres, where the church and refuge nestle under a primeval overhanging massif.

need to know
ⓦwww.parks.it/parco.nazionale.gran.paradiso
ⓦwww.pngp.it
ⓦwww.granparadiso.net

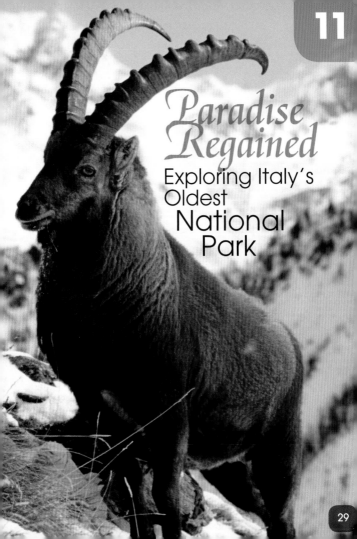

Paradise Regained

Exploring Italy's Oldest National Park

For years I had watched Stromboli from my house on the island of Salina. It's the most active volcano in Europe, and on clear nights, even from a distance of 40km, I would see its worms of red lava glowing in the dark. If there was any place on earth where mankind was not meant to go, surely it was the crater of an active volcano. And yet the lure was irresistible.

The steady, three-hour climb to the top proved not to be difficult. We passed through the rich aromas of the maquis that eminated from the wild roses, fig trees, prickly pears and clumps of capers all around us. The sky was clear, the sea blue and the breathtaking view spanned from Mount Etna to Calabria. I was wondering what I'd been scared of, when a resounding clash, like an iron door slamming shut, reminded me. I jumped. Mario the guide turned round: "Don't worry, it's normal". I tried to look as though walking up an erupting volcano were the most natural thing in the world.

Abruptly, the vegetation ended. The ground beneath our feet turned to sand, strewn with small jagged boulders spewed out by the volcano. We stopped to don heavy clothes and helmets, and follow the final ridge to the top. There was a freezing northern wind.

At the top, all I could see were clouds of white steam. Then, suddenly, they glowed a fierce, translucent red as four spouts of fire threw up a fountain of glowing boulders that drew tracks of red light across the night sky. Mario chose that moment to start talking on the radio. A sudden, panicked thought: we were in danger. But no, this was Stromboli, and things were normal – he was discussing dinner.

need to know

Climbing Stromboli is permitted only with a registered guide, who will be in constant radio contact with the volcanologists at Stromboli's observatory. Ascents are timed so you reach the summit at sunset. Even when it's warm in town, it will be freezing on the summit; take warm clothes, water, food and a torch. You're provided with helmets. Contact Magmatrek, Via Vittorio Emanuele, in Stromboli (@www.magmatrek.it) for further

Getting shaken and stirred on Stromboli's slopes

12

13

Alba's White Gold: *Snuffling for Truffles* in Piemonte

One of Italy's great seasonal events is the autumn truffle season, when Italian gastronomes descend upon the historic town of Alba in search of the white Piemontese *tartufo* or truffle. The *tuber magnatum pico*, as it's known, develops in cool damp chalky soil 10–15 cm underground, and is only found in this part of Piemonte. Local farmers use specially trained dogs or *tabui* (literally 'bastards') to sniff them out in the oak and hazelnut forests near Alba, usually at night – not only because the whole thing is tremendously secretive but also because fully mature truffles are said to emit a stronger perfume after dark.

On the final weekend in October, the market for truffles in Alba's old centre, is at its peak. Once inside the covered venue, the experience is a sensory overload. Never again will you whiff so many truffles – or truffle products – in such a confined space. However, buying one of these little gastronomic gems can be stressful. Prices are steep – £2300–3500 a kilo – and the market traders as sharp as they come. They'll happily let you pick up and smell as many truffles as you wish, but learning how to discern a decent truffle's characteristics isn't easy. Observe the locals. Truffles must be consumed within ten days of their discovery: they should be brownish-white in colour and clean of dirt – greyish truffles are old truffles. They should be firm to the touch and knobbly in texture; a spongy truffle must be eaten that day or not at all. Look out also for any holes which might have been filled with dirt to increase the weight. Above all, be sure to smell the truffle thoroughly: a mature specimen will possess a strong and nutty bouquet. If you feel the need for a second opinion, the "Quality Commission" in the centre of the market will take a look for you. You might think they would shave off a small piece. But that's not needed. All they do is remove the truffle from the paper towel, place it on the scales, test the firmness between the thumb and index finger, and, finally, put it as close to the nose as physically possible and SNIFF. Once authenticated, the truffle is placed in a numbered paper bag. Is it really worth all the hype? Well, the taste is sensual, earthy and curiously moreish, whether it's shaved thinly over pasta, or as the basis of various oils, cream sauces and butters. And where else could you get to eat something quite so expensive?

need to know

The truffle season runs from the end of September to the beginning of November, and Alba celebrates with its own fair for gourmets. The town's truffle market is held every weekend during the month of October, between 8am and 8pm. More information can be found at @www.tuber.it

Siena's famous bareback horserace – Il Palio – is a highly charged, death-defying dash around the boundary of the city's majestic Piazza del Campo. It's also likely to be the most rabidly partisan event you'll ever witness. Twice every summer riders elected by each of the city's ancient districts – the contrade – compete in a bid to win the much prized "Palio" or banner. Sounds like fun? It is. But the Palio is not just a bit of tourist fluff. On the two days that the race takes place – as well as throughout the exacting year-long preparations – the Sienese are playing for very high stakes indeed, and the air positively crackles with the seriousness of it all.

There's a parade around the piazza at 5pm, with banner hurlers – bandierai – from each contrada, accompanied by the chimes of the bell-tower, after which the square is a riot of colour until the "War Chariot", drawn by two pairs of white oxen, displays the prize for the coming contest. The race itself takes only ninety seconds to complete, and the only rule is that there are no rules: practically any sort of violence toward rival riders or animals is permitted, and anything short of directly interfering with another jockey's reins or flinging a rider to the ground is seen as fair game. Each jockey carries a special whip or nerbo – by tradition fashioned from the skin of a bull's penis and thus thought to give a particularly deep sting, not to mention conferring super-potency on its wielder. The course is so treacherous, with its sharp turns and sloping, slippery surfaces that often fewer than half the participants finish. But in any case it's only the horse that matters – the beast that crosses the line first (even without its rider), is the winner, after which the residents of the victorious district sing, dance and celebrate their victory into the small hours.

34

14

Playing for High Stakes at Siena's Palio

need to know The race begins early evening at 7.45pm on July 2 and 7pm on August 16. To see anything, you need to stake your claim at least by lunchtime in the standing-room-only area of the piazza, where a spot at the edge of the course offers the best thrill. If money's no object @www.initaly.com/ads/palio/palio.htm has information on how to get tickets for the limited seating available – prices start at over €300.

Pity the poor folk picking through the rubble of the Forum in Rome. To make the most of the ruins there you have to use your imagination. In the ancient Roman resort town of Pompeii, however, it's a little easier. Pompeii was famously buried by Vesuvius in 79AD, and the result is perhaps the best-preserved Roman town anywhere, with a street plan that is easy to discern not to mention wander – and a number of palatial villas that are still largely intact. It's crowded, not surprisingly, but is a large site, and it's quite possible to escape the hordes and experience

Solving the Mysteries of

the strangely still quality of Pompeii, sitting around ancient swimming pools, peering at frescoes and mosaics still in situ, standing behind the counters of ancient shops.

Finish up your visit at the incredible Villa of Mysteries, a suburban dwelling just outside the ancient city. Its layout is much the same as the other villas of the city, but its walls are decorated with a cycle of frescoes that give a unique insight into the ancient world – and most importantly they are viewable in situ, unlike most of the rest of Pompeii's mosaics and frescoes, which have found their way to Naples' archeological museum. No one can be sure what these pictures represent, but it's thought that they show the initiation rites of a young woman preparing for marriage. Set against deep ruby-red backgrounds, and full of marvellously preserved detail, they are dramatic and universal works, showing the initiate's progress from naïve young girl to eligible young woman. But above all they tell a story – one that speaks to us loud and clear from 79AD.

Pompeii

15

need to know
Pompeii is open in summer every day from 8.30am until 6pm; in winter it closes at 3.30pm. It costs €10 to get in. Like all of Italy's most popular sights, try to go out of season, when it can feel as if you've got the place to yourself – a rare and very evocative treat.

he ancient hilltown, with its crumbling houses and belltowers rising above a landscape of vineyards and olive groves, is one of the quintessential images of Italy, and nowhere in the country provides more photogenic examples than the area around Siena.

The Chianti region, immediately to the north of Siena, has numerous pretty little hill-towns, with Castellina in Chianti making the obvious target for a half-day trip. Equally close is Colle di Val d'Elsa – the industrial zone of the lower town mars the view a little, but the upper town is a real gem. The most famous of all the Sienese satellites, however, is San Gimignano, whose tower-filled skyline is one of Europe's great medieval urban landscapes. On the downside, in high season the narrow lanes of San Gimignano get as busy as London's Oxford Street, so if you're touring in summer and don't relish the crowds, head instead to windswept Volterra, a dramatically situated place whose Etruscan origins are never far from the surface. Like Pitigliano, in the far south of Tuscany, Volterra is more a clifftop settlement than a hill-town – walk just a few

76 Touring the Tuscan hilltowns

minutes from the cathedral and you'll come upon the Balze, a sheer wall of rock down which a fair chunk of Volterra has tumbled over the centuries.

Some 40km south of Siena lies Montalcino, as handsome a hill-town as you could hope to find: famed for the mighty red wines produced in the surrounding vineyards, it's also very close to the ancient abbey of Sant'Antimo, one of Tuscany's most beautiful churches. From Montalcino you could loop to the even more handsome Montepulciano, which is ranged along a narrow ridge and strewn with Renaissance palaces – and is the home of another renowned wine, the Vino Nobile di Montepulciano. East of here, on other side of the river plain known as the Valdichiana, lofty Cortona is reached by a five-kilometre road that winds up from the valley floor through terraces of vines and olives. Clinging so closely to the slopes that there's barely a horizontal street in the centre, Cortona commands a gorgeous panorama: climb to the summit of the town at night and you'll see the villages of southern Tuscany twinkling like ships' lights on a dark sea.

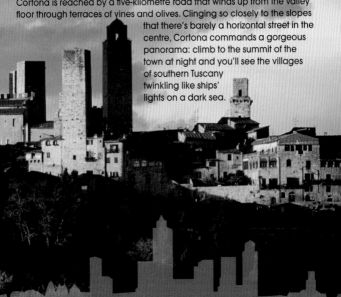

need to know
There are regular bus connections between Siena and San Gimignano, Volterra, Montalcino and Montepulciano. Cortona is most easily reached from Arezzo, Castellina from Florence and Colle di Val d'Elsa from Volterra.

Baroque around the Clock
braving the midday sun in Lecce

In a mid-August heatwave, the heel of Italy is not a place many people would choose to be. Still less standing in the centre of Lecce's Piazza del Duomo, a heatsink square paved with burning stone flags, surrounded by burning stone buildings and overlooked by a sun that seems as hard and unrelenting as the stone itself. In such conditions the day begins at thirty degrees, and rises smoothly through the forties before topping out a temperature that should be measured in gas marks, you feel, not degrees centigrade.

Squinting up at the towering stone façade of the Duomo and the adjacent bishop's palace, however, it all starts to make sense. Here, and on the surfaces of churches and palaces all over the city, the stone breaks out in exuberant encrustations, as if the very heat had caused the underlying architecture to boil over into fantastical shapes and accretions.

In fact, it wasn't the heat which caused Lecce's stone to crawl with decoration. It was a rare combination of time and place. The city lies beside a unique outcrop of soft sandstone in the razor-hard limestone that forms the tip of the heel of the Italian boot – and stonemason's chisels take to this *pietra Leccese* like hot knives to butter. And at the very time the masons were setting to work, in the early sixteenth century, the stagey ornamentation of the Baroque style was taking hold in Italy. Lecce, the city they call the Florence of the South, was the fervid, sunstruck result.

need to know The tourist office is at 24 via Vittorio Emanuele (℡0832.332.463, ⓦwww.pugliaturismo. com). The grand **Risorgimento**, via Augusto Imperatore (℡0832.242.125, ⓦwww.webshop.it/hotelrisorgimento), is an excellent place to stay.

The west front of the Basilica di Santa Croce, a few steps from the Duomo, spews out such an abundance of vegetation and grotesque animal life that it as if the vitality of the sun-warmed land had found expression in sculpture.

Shopping with style in Milan

milan

is synonymous with shopping: boutiques from all the world's top clothes and accessory designers are within a hop, skip and a high-heeled teeter from each other. The atmosphere is snooty, the labels elitist and the experience priceless.

The city has been associated with top-end fashion since the 1970s, when local designers broke with the staid atmosphere of Italy's traditional fashion home, the Palazzo Pitti in Florence. It was during the 1980s, however, that the worldwide thirst for designer labels consolidated the international reputation of home-grown talent such as Armani, Gucci, Prada, Versace and Dolce & Gabana.

You don't need to be rich to feel part of it. These days the stores themselves make almost as important a statement as the clothes. In-house cafés are springing up, as are exhibition spaces, even barber's and spas. Even if you're not in the market for splashing out, you can still indulge yourself without breaking the bank: for a handful of euros you can sip a cocktail at Bar Martini, in the Dolce & Gabbana flagship store at Corso Venezia 15; enjoy an espresso and a monogrammed chocolate at the Gucci Café inside Milan's famous nineteenth-century Galleria Vittorio Emanuele II; or, perhaps, drink prosecco at the tables outside the Armani Café, at Via Manzoni 31, part of the four-storey temple to all things Giorgio. And, as you're here for the experience, why not head for the ultimate in bling at Just Cavalli Food, in Via della Spiga, where the leopardskin-clad clientele floats down in a cloud-lift to the boutique's café, which is lined with a saltwater aquarium swimming with brightly coloured tropical fish.

need to know

The top-name fashion stores are concentrated just northeast of Milan's cathedral in the rectangle of streets and cobbled lanes known as the "Quadrilatero d'Oro" or the "Golden Quadrilateral". Most shops in central Milan open Tuesday to Saturday 10am to 7pm plus Monday afternoons, although most are now also open on Monday mornings and even Sunday afternoons. The summer sales usually last from early July through August, while the winter ones start around the second week of January and last for a month.

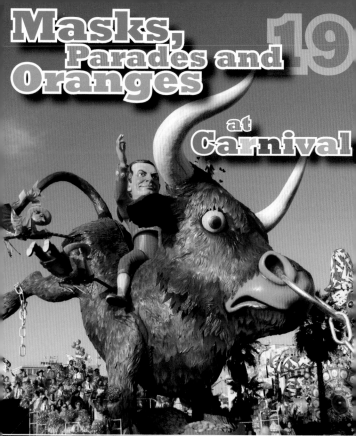

Masks, Parades and Oranges

at Carnival

You don't necessarily think of Italy when it comes to carnival celebrations. But there are three Italian cities that take carnival very seriously indeed...

need to know @www.carnivalofvenice.com; @www.viareggio.ilcarnevale.com
– tickets cost €13; @www.carnevalediivrea.it

Venice is the best-known, and as a setting for a carnival, utterly unique – here carnival floats do literally that, gliding along on the water itself rather than chugging down the road on the back of a truck. The maze of narrow pedestrian streets and interlaced canals are a source of discovery at every turn – all the more so if you're kitted out in a fancy costume or, at the very least, a mask – and ultimately, the sheer visual delight of the city, and the tangible feeling that somehow you are adrift on an island in some parallel universe, make carnival here an experience like no other.

Viareggio on the Tuscan coast has been hosting one of Europe's liveliest carnivals for over a century. For four consecutive Sundays leading up to Lent there's an amazing parade of floats that would pass muster in some of the best Brazilian events, although Viareggio is probably best-known for its carri – giant, lavishly designed papier-maché models of politicians and celebrities that give a great idea of who's hot and who's not each year. Many celebs come to Viareggio just to clock how they've been depicted, and each parade ends with a huge fireworks display, with Viareggio's bars and clubs buzzing for some time after.

Carnival is also celebrated in Ivrea, not far from Turin. Although it gets underway weeks before, things get really interesting on the Sunday before Shrove Tuesday – the town fills with revellers who tuck into bowls of beans ladled out from giant cauldrons in the main square before taking part in a humungous orange fight, which starts at the same time each afternoon for the next three days. Anyone and anything is fair game here, and by the end of each day everyone is covered in pulp and drenched in freshly-squeezed juice; there's nowhere to walk that's not swimming in vitamin C, and the air is full of the bitter smell of oranges. On Shrove Tuesday it finishes with a huge procession and a celebratory bonfire in the square.

Hiking through the steep hills north of Bergamo, not far from Milan, you'll notice an eerie silence. After a while it dawns on you that the reason is there is no birdsong. People around here traditionally love to hunt, and until recently one of the staples of the local cuisine was *polenta e osei* – or polenta with small birds: traditionally larks or thrushes skewered whole and roasted and served over cornmeal that is slow-cooked to a creamy mash. This dish is considered a cruel affair nowadays, not least because the birds were often roasted while still alive, so it's rare that you'll get the opportunity to taste it outside someone's home; and in any case you might not relish scoffing the birds whole, beak and all, as you are supposed to. But Bergamo remains one of Italy's great food cities, and you can still find *osei scapai*, literally 'birds that got away', served with the same yellow polenta – which is a staple of the town to the extent that its inhabitants are known to the rest of Italy as *polentoni*. The "birds", though, are nowadays a mixed grill of veal, bacon and chicken livers cooked up with fresh sage and then roasted in the oven. Just as delicious, and a lot easier to eat!

need to know
Bergamo is easily reached by train, and also has its own international airport, Milan-Bergamo/Orio al Serio. **Donizetti** is at Via Gombito 17a, **Da Mimmo** at Via Colleoni 17 and **Caffè Funicolare** on Piazza Mercato delle Scarpe. All are closed on Tuesday.

Feasting in Bergamo

Bergamo is perfect for a foodie weekend. Rambling up narrow, cobbled Via Gombito, the pedestrianized main street of Bergamo's Upper Town, you're drawn in by the profusion of greengrocers, cavernous *salumerie* festooned with all kinds of cured meats and mustily fragrant cheese shops. Sit under the streetside loggia at *Donizetti* and have a *degustazione* platter of *prosciutto*, *bresaola* (wafer-thin slices of air-dried beef) and goose sausage, along with gorgonzola and spicy bagoss cheese, washed down with sparkling *Franciacorta* wine. Take in an evening meal at *Da Mimmo*, a family-run restaurant where you can opt for *casoncelli*, ravioli stuffed with sausagemeat, sage and butter, or flavourful rabbit stew, served with – what else? – polenta. Don't miss dessert either, especially as it gives you the chance to savour more fake birds in another version of *polenta e osei* – basically sponge cake topped with tiny marzipan larks. Round things off with a post-prandial coffee at the *Caffè Funicolare*, at the top of the funicular station that links the upper and lower town. From here the view over Bergamo is stupendous, looking south towards Milan. But with food this good, who needs Milan?

on the trail of *Caravaggio*

21 **in Rome**

With his dark, dramatic paintings and violent, hell-raising private life, no other Italian artist captures the modern imagination quite as much as **Michelangelo Merisi da Caravaggio**. Perhaps it was his **rock-and-roll lifestyle**, or maybe it's the sheer narrative force of his paintings – which were considered at the time as at best unseemly, or at worst downright sacrilegious. Viewed now, his work still packs quite a punch; so it's no surprise to learn that Caravaggio's reputation at the time was one of hell-raiser and maverick.

There's no better place to track down some of Caravaggio's best works than in his adopted home town of Rome. And what's more, many of the paintings you can see here are still in the churches for which they were commissioned. The trail starts bang in the centre of the city, where the church of San Luigi dei Francesi is home to the **Calling of St Matthew**, a typically dramatic piece of work, depicting the tax collector Matthew in the sort of rough-and-ready tavern environment that Caravaggio would have understood well – counting money, and looking up in surprise as he is called away from his companions. Ten minutes' walk north from here, the church of Santa Maria del Popolo has two paintings hung side by side, one showing the **Conversion of St Paul** – bathed in beatific light under his horse on the road to Damascus – and the other the **Crucifixion of St Peter**, with muscular henchmen hauling the elderly but clearly weighty bulk of St Peter onto his upside-down cross. These are powerful paintings, and looking at them up close like this you almost feel that you are intruding into a private moment. Indeed, it's maybe no surprise that they have been dubbed the most revolutionary works in the whole history of sacred art – a tag that could also be applied to the **Madonna of the Pilgrims** in the church of Sant'Agostino, which shows the virgin as an ordinary Roman woman, standing in a typically shabby doorway, adored by dirty pilgrims in tattered clothes.

Caravaggio's work peppers Roman galleries too, and you should also stop by the Galleria Borghese, where a small collection of his paintings includes his last work, **David with the Head of Goliath**, painted while on the run from Rome for murder, and oddly prescient of the artist's own death. It's not a joyful painting: David holds the head of Goliath away from him in disgust, and the scene is one of sorrow rather than triumph. Most tellingly, it's believed that the bloody, severed head is a self-portrait of Caravaggio himself; and gazing at the anguished, bearded face feels like staring across the centuries into the artist's soul.

need to know
San Luigi dei Francesi Via della Scrofa.
Santa Maria del Popolo Piazza del Popolo.
Sant'Agostino Piazza Sant'Agostino.
Museo e Galleria Borghese Tues–Sun 9am–7pm; €8.50; booking obligatory on ☎06.328.10 or ⊛www.galleriaborghese.it

The Amalfi Coast, playground of the rich and famous, exudes Italian chic. The landscape is breathtakingly dramatic: sheer craggy cliffs plunge down to meet the water which is a shimmering, cerulean blue and tiny secluded coves dot the coastline, accessible only by very expensive yacht. Setting off down the coastal road you can't help but fancy yourself a bit of a jetsetter.

The drive itself deserves celebrity status; you may think you've seen coastal roads, but this one's in a class of its own, hewn into the sides of the mountain and barely wide enough for two large cars to pass comfortably, let alone the gargantuan buses that whiz between the main towns. On one side rises an impenetrable wall of mountain, while on the other there's nothing but a sheer, unforgiving drop to the sea. Overcome the instinct to hide your head in your hands, and embrace the exhilaration – this is not a ride to miss. The road snakes it way along the side of the mountain, plunging headlong into dark, roughly-hewn tunnels, curving sharply around headlands, and traversing the odd crevice on the way. Every hair-raising bend presents you with yet another sweeping vista.

Don't get so caught up in the drive that you forget to stop and enjoy the calm beauty of the effortlessly exclusive coastal towns. Explore the posh cliffside town of Positano or stroll the peaceful promenades and piazzas of elegant hilltop Ravello. And in more down-to-earth Amalfi, just below, re-adjust to the languorous pace of resort-town life at a café before heading off to enjoy the town's sandy beach. Presided over by a towering cathedral adorned with glittering gold tiles and a lush and peaceful cloister, it's the perfect antidote to the adrenaline rush of the Amalfi Drive.

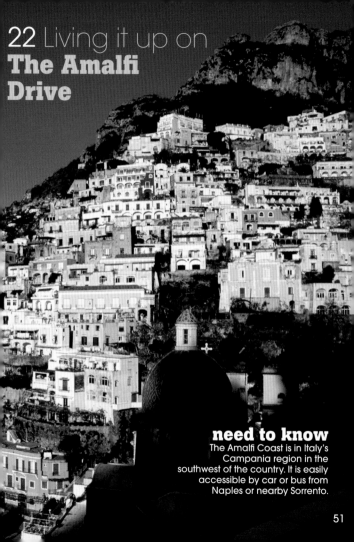

22 Living it up on
The Amalfi Drive

need to know

The Amalfi Coast is in Italy's Campania region in the southwest of the country. It is easily accessible by car or bus from Naples or nearby Sorrento.

23

Looking for Pasta Heaven

It may be just a simple combination of basic ingredients – flour, water and sometimes eggs – but pasta is the food that most defines Italy. It's **one of the most versatile foods** you could imagine, and is eaten all over the country – although it is in fact the basic staple of the South. There are **hundreds of pasta shapes and sizes**, each designed for a certain kind of sauce, and it's testimony to its importance in the Italian diet that each shape is identified according to a nationally recognised numbering system. **Spaghetti** is the best-known and most versatile; tubular **rigatoni** and shell-like **conchiglie** are great vehicles for ragù or meat sauce, as are Bolognese **tagliatelle** noodles, while thick **papardelle** are perfect foils for porcini mushrooms and thick gamey sauces. Like most Italian cooking, pasta is best at its simplest, cooked with lots of liberally salted water and taken out at precisely the right moment and served al dente – ie not soft, but with a bite – and then combined with the freshest possible ingredients.

What you eat depends – as ever in Italy – on where you are in the country. Everything is regional. It's hard to find a restaurant in Liguria that doesn't serve **pasta al pesto**, usually with *trofie* – short, fat pellets of pasta and potato – and with a few green beans and boiled potatoes. Most eateries in Rome serve **spaghetti all carbonara** – with raw eggs and bacon; **bucatini cacio e pepe** – thick hollow noodles with pepper and lots of pecorino cheese; or **all'amatriciana** – with tomatoes and smoked bacon. In Bologna you will usually find lots of filled pasta alternatives like **agnolotti**, **tortellini** and **ravioli**. But the city that is renowned for the best pasta is Naples, and it's here that you'll get the closest to pasta heaven. They claim the water down here improves the quality of the pasta, and the sauces are simple yet hearty: **spaghetti alle vongole**, with tomatoes, lots of garlic and baby clams – and, perhaps the simplest and most ubiquitous Italian dish of them all, **spaghetti al pomodoro**, with tomatoes, garlic and a little fresh basil. "The angels in paradise", once opined the mayor of Naples, "eat nothing but pasta al pomodoro". And after eating spaghetti in Naples, you might be forced to agree.

need to know
Da Genio Salita San Leonardo 61r, Genova ☎010.588.443
Matricianella, Via del Leone 2, Roma ☎06.683.2100.
Bellini, Via Santa Maria di Constaninopoli 80, Napoli ☎081.459.774

Several European cities hold major contemporary art fairs, but the leader of the pack is the **Venice Biennale**, an event that has more glamour, prestige and news value than any other cultural jamboree. Nowadays it's **associated with the cutting edge**, but it hasn't always been that way. First held in 1895 as the city's contribution to the celebrations for the silver wedding anniversary of King Umberto I and Margherita of Savoy, in its early years it was essentially a showcase for salon painting.

Since World War II, however, the Biennale has become **a self-consciously avant-garde event**, a transformation symbolized by the award of the major Biennale prize in 1964 to Robert Rauschenberg, one of the enfants terribles of the American art scene. The French contingent campaigned vigorously against the nomination of this New World upstart, and virtually every Biennale since then has been **characterized by controversy** of some sort.

After decades of occurring in even-numbered years, the Biennale shifted back to being **held every odd-numbered year from June to November** so that the centenary show could be held in 1995. The main site is in the **Giardini Pubblici**, where there are permanent pavilions for about forty countries that participate every time, plus space for a thematic international exhibition. **The pavilions are a show in themselves**, forming a unique colony that features work by some of the great names of modern architecture and design: the Austrian pavilion, for example, was built by the Secession architect Josef Hoffman in the 1930s, and the Finnish pavilion was created by Alvar Aalto in the 1950s. Naturally enough, the biggest pavilion is the Italian one – it's five times larger than the next largest.

The central part of the Biennale is supplemented by **exhibitions in venues that are normally closed to the public**. This is another big attraction of the event – only during the Biennale are you likely to see the **colossal Corderie in the Arsenale** (the former rope-factory) or the huge salt warehouses over on the Zàttere. In addition, various sites throughout the city (including the streets) host **fringe exhibitions, installations and performances**, particularly in the opening weeks. And with artists, critics and collectors swarming around the bars and restaurants, the artworld buzz of the Biennale penetrates every corner of Venice.

need to know Information on tickets and other Biennale practicalities – as well as the Venice Film Festival – is available at ⓦwww.labiennale.org.

Celebrating
the Biennale

Gorgeous bays and smouldering volcanoes, boisterous markets and fabulous food, Sicily has the lot. But what is less well-known is the fact that, amid the energy and chaos of the contemporary island, it is also home to some of Italy's oldest and most perfectly preserved classical sites. What's more, the most historic places on Sicily are usually the most sublimely located – isolated specimens of classical civilization where you come face to face with a distant era of heroism, hedonism and unforgiving gods. Joining their dots is a fun and evocative way to explore the island.

Starting in the far west of Sicily, the fifth century BC Greek temple of Segesta, secluded on a hilltop west of Palermo, enjoys perhaps the most magnificent location of all, the skeletal symmetery of its Doric temple and brilliantly sited theatre giving views right across the bay – not to mention the *autostrada* snaking far below. Further east, just outside the south coast town of Agrigento, there are more Doric temples, this time from a century earlier and dramatically arrayed along a ridge overlooking the sea. They would have been the imposing setting for inscrutable and often blood-curdling ceremonies – and yet you can walk a bit further and you're back in the Catholic present (at the tiny Norman church of San Biagio). Inland from here, leap forward almost 1000 years and you're still only in the Roman era,

viewing the vivid mosaics of the Villa Romana just outside Piazza Armerina – sumptuous works that date from the fourth century AD and show manly Romans snaring tigers, ostriches and elephants, and a delightful children's hunt with the kids being chased by their prey (don't worry – they're only hares and peacocks).

Classical Studies
in Sicily

need to know

Information and tickets for performances are available from the tourist offices at Taormina (wwww.gate2taormina.com) and Siracusa (wwww.apt-siracusa.it).

Then, on the east coast, there are the marvellous theatres of Taormina and Siracusa. The former once staged gladiatorial combats and is now the scene of perhaps the most stirringly sited arts performances in the world, with views that encompass sparkling seas and Europe's friskiest volcano, Mount Etna – usually topped by a menacing plume of smoke.

Siracusa's Greek Theatre is one of the biggest and best preserved of all classical auditoriums, and although it lacks the panoramic panache of Taormina, its grander scale more than makes up for it. It's used every summer for concerts and Greek drama, and a starlit evening at either theatre is the perfect way to round off your classical tour.

Ultimate
experiences
Italy
miscellany

 **Food**

Modern pizza was created in Naples in the early nineteenth century – the first **Pizza Margherita** was baked in the 1890s for Queen Margherita of Savoy.

▶▶ Top ten regional specialties

Bagna Cauda A Piemontese sauce of oil, butter, anchovies and garlic, served like a fondue.

Gorgonzola One of the great Italian cheeses, hailing from Lombardy, blue-veined and either creamy (dolce) or sharp (piccante).

Mozzarella di Bufala You may have tasted mozzarella before, but nothing gets close to the real buffalo-milk version from the Campania. Another of Italy's great cheeses.

Parmigiano-Reggiano This hard cheese, commonly known as parmesan, comes from the area around Parma and Reggio-Emilia, and its production goes back to at least the early medieval period. Probably the best-known and most versatile Italian cheese of them all.

Pesto alla Genovese *The* Ligurian pasta sauce, made from basil, olive oil, garlic, parmesan and pine nuts.

Porchetta Basically roast pork, with lots of stuffing and crackling, and sold from open-air stalls in Umbria, Tuscany and Lazio.

Prosciutto di San Daniele The greatest of the great cured hams from Parma and around.

Saltimbocca alla Romana Veal with prosciutto and sage, cooked in marsala – a Roman dish.

Tiramisù Treviso's scrumptious coffee dessert.

Truffles Italy produces twenty percent of all black truffles, a delicacy of Umbria, and virtually all white truffles (from Piedmont).

▶▶ Top Italian restaurants

Restaurant magazine featured four Italian restaurants in its Top 50 in 2006:

Gambero Rosso, San Vincenzo (Livorno). Modern Tuscan cooking, with sumptuous fresh seafood and shellfish.

Enoteca Pinchiorri, Florence. Great Tuscan food and old-fashioned elegance.

Le Calandre, Padua. Modern Italian food bang in the heart of Padua.

Dal Pescatore, Canneto. This family-owned restaurant between Cremona and Mantua blends traditional and modern Italian cuisine.

"We shall feast our grape-gleaners with lasagne so tempting to swallow in slippery ropes."

Robert Browning

 Transport

Vespa (meaning "wasp") started manufacturing scooters in 1946. They gradually assumed iconic status in Italy (Audrey Hepburn rode one in *Roman Holiday*) and also in the UK, where (along with **Lambretta**) they became associated with the Mods youth culture in the 1960s. The UK is still its second largest market after Italy.

Ferrari, established in 1929, and **Lamborghini**, established in 1963 but now owned by Audi, make the most sought-after, expensive sports cars in the world: the Ferrari 250 GTO (1962–64) was voted the best sports car of all time by *Sports Car International* in 2004, and fetches $5–9 million today. A new Ferrari costs around U$250,000.

Fiat owns 85 percent of Ferrari (along with **Maserati** and **Alfa Romeo**) and is still Italy's largest carmaker: the Turin-based manufacturer is the world's tenth largest according to *Fortune* magazine, and the third-largest company in Italy based on revenue (the largest is insurance firm Assicurazioni Generali).

Explorers

Christopher Columbus (1451–1506) "discovered" the New World for Spain in 1492, but always claimed to be Italian, born in Genoa. Columbus Day (October 12) is still proudly celebrated in the US by Italian-Americans.

Columbus was inspired by the tales of **Marco Polo** (1254–1324), a Venetian merchant, who claimed he had spent seventeen years working for Kublai Khan, the Emperor of China in his book *Il Milione* (*The Travels of Marco Polo*).

 Religion

The Pope is regarded as the successor of St Peter, who was martyred in Rome by Nero (64 AD) along with St Paul; he can choose any official name but Peter. Out of a total 265 popes, 217 have been Italian. The last was Pope John Paul I, who ruled for just 33 days in 1978.

▶▶ Italy's holiest sites

St Peter's Basilica, Rome/Vatican City. Built over the crucifixion spot of St Peter, this is the world's largest and most visited church.

Duomo, Turin. Home to the Turin Shroud, said to have covered the body of Jesus before his resurrection, and housed in its own chapel (though shown only on special occasions).

Basilica di San Francesco, Assisi. The church built in memory of one of the great Christian saints, St Francis (1182-1226), patron saint of animals and Italy from 1939, who lived in Assisi all his life.

San Giovanni Rotondo, near Foggia, Puglia. Home of the revered priest and now saint, Padre Pio, who died in 1968, and now a massive pilgrimage centre.

▶▶ The Romans

Constantine legalized Christianity in 313, but the Romans had their own pagan religion based on the Greek gods:

Roman Gods	Role	Greek name
Jupiter	King of the gods	Zeus
Juno	Queen of the gods	Hera
Neptune	God of the sea	Poseidon
Bacchus	God of wine	Dionysus
Mars	God of war	Ares
Venus	Goddess of love	Aphrodite
Apollo	God of sun, light and festivities	Apollo
Mercury	Messenger of the gods	Hermes
Minerva	Goddess of wisdom	Athena
Pluto	God of the underworld	Hades

Football

English workers brought **football** to Italy in the 1890s, with James Richardson Spensley establishing Genoa in 1896, and Alfred Edwards AC Milan three years later; both clubs still incorporate the cross of St George in their team badges. Italy's **national team** (known as the "Azzurri" for their dark blue shirts) went on to win the World Cup four times (1934, 1938, 1982 and 2006). Italy's clubs have won 27 major European trophies, more than any other nation. Their Serie A is one of the best leagues in the world, despite being rocked by a match-fixing scandal in 2006. The league is traditionally dominated by AC Milan and Internazionale (also from Milan), and Juventus from Turin (historically Italy's most successful team), although the two principal Rome teams, Roma and Lazio, are also among the biggies these days.

Wine

Italy has been making wine for over 4000 years and produces around five million litres annually, which was second only to France in 2005.

▶▶ Top ten Italian wines

Barolo Piemonte wine that is one of the great Italian reds, very smooth when aged.

Brunella di Montalcino Rich complex red wine from Tuscany – can be very expensive.

Chianti Classico Italy's most famous red wine, originating in Tuscany and made from Sangiovese grapes.

Dolcetta d'Alba Purpley-red wine from Piemonte.

Frascati Light dry white from southern Lazio – much better in Italy than abroad.

Lambrusco Slightly effervescent red from the Emilia-Romagna region that is great if drunk locally, terrible anywhere else.

Montepulciano d'Abruzzo Abruzzo's most avidly consumed red.

Salice Salentino Smooth and full-bodied Puglia red.

Soave Crisp, dry white wine from the Veneto.

Valpolicella The most celebrated red wine of the Veneto.

 **Cinema**

▶▶ Italy on film

The English Patient (1996). Based on the Michael Ondaatje book, this is set in part in a tranquil Italian villa.

Room with a View (1984). Merchant & Ivory classic of EM Forster's novel, half set in early twentieth-century Florence.

The Talented Mr Ripley (1999). A disturbing tale of deception, obsession and murder, set in Venice, Rome and along the coast near Naples.

Tea with Mussolini (1999). Set in Florence, this concerns a group of English and American women who bring up a local boy, disowned by his father.

Under the Tuscan Sun (2005). Based on the book by Frances Mayes, and following the exploits of a New Yorker looking for love in Tuscany.

▶▶ Italian movies

Bicycle Thieves (1948). This neo-realist classic is many people's favourite film of all time.

Dear Diary (1993). Set partly in Rome, partly in the Aeolian islands, Nanni Moretti is Italy's Woody Allen in this wry commentary on modern life.

Death in Venice (1971). Luchino Visconti's film of Thomas Mann's book goes for the jugular in this Mahler-drenched emotional epic.

La Dolce Vita (1960). Federico Fellini's most celebrated film, satirizing the vacuity of the Sixties era.

Cinema Paradiso (1989). A big hit internationally, this is the touching tale of a famous film director returning home to his Sicilian village.

Hands Over the City (1963). Francesco Rosi's searing critique of developers and the mob in 1960s Naples.

Life is Beautiful (1997). A World War II tragicomedy that introduced Roberto Benigni to an international audience, and to an Oscar.

Novecento (1976). Bertolucci's six-hour epic follows the lives of two groups of men during the rise of fascism and the outbreak of war.

Il Postino (1994). Set in 1950s Italy, this is the heart-warming story of a postman who comes to love the poetry of Pablo Neruda.

Rome Open City (1945). One of the finest movies of the neo-realist director, Roberto Rossellini, evoking the capital in the last days of the German occupation.

> *"A man who has not been in Italy, is always conscious of an inferiority, from his not having seen what it is expected a man should see."*
> **Samuel Johnson**

Top ten fashion houses

Dolce et Gabbana, Milan, 1985
Fendi, Rome, 1918
Giorgio Armani, Milan, 1975
Gucci, Florence, 1921
Max Mara, Reggio Amilia, 1951
Moschino, Milan, 1983
Prada, Milan, 1913
Salvatore Ferragamo, Florence, 1925
Valentino, Rome, 1959
Versace, Milan, 1978

Inventions

Galileo Galilei (1564–1642) was born in Pisa and is regarded as the father of modern astronomy and science, making major breakthroughs in scientific method and theory, improving the telescope and discovering several of Jupiter's moons.

Language

Latin was the language of the Romans and became the *lingua franca* of most of Europe in the Middle Ages – it was the official language of the Roman Catholic church until the 1960s. The **Romance** languages, spoken by more than 600 million people, are derived from Latin: French, Italian, Spanish, Albanian, Romanian, Catalan and Portuguese.

Italy's ten best hotels

Bauer il Palazzo, Venice. This boutique hotel in Venice enjoys an unbeatable location in a grand palazzo on the Grand Canal.

Byblos Art Hotel Villa Amista, (Negarine) Verona. This fifteenth-century palace houses Italy's coolest modern-design hotel, crammed full of art and cutting-edge furniture.

Caruso, Ravello. There are some great hotels with dramatic locations up in Ravello, but this is probably the best of the lot.

Grand Hotel a Villa Feltrinelli, Gargnano. A sumptuous palace dating from 1892 and beautifully restored, right on the shore of Lake Garda.

Grotta Palazzese, Polignano a Mare. Carved into a cliff facing the Adriatic, this hotel enjoys a totally captivating location, and has an amazing grotto restaurant.

Hotel de Russie, Rome. This could just be the capital's best-located and most luxurious hotel, with a fantastic courtyard garden in which to sip Bellini cocktails – which were incidentally invented here.

Punta Tragara, Capri. Where better to stay on Capri, high above the Faraglioni rocks, and with a stunning poolside restaurant.

San Domenico Palace, Taormina. Another monastery turned hotel, with views of Etna and Taormina's ancient theatre.

Villa d'Este, Como. This sixteenth-century villa sits right by the lake and is surrounded by acres of sumptuous gardens.

Villa San Michele, Fiesole. Set in a fifteenth-century monastery, this small luxury hotel just outside Florence is pure class.

 # History

According to legend, Rome was founded by **Romulus** and **Remus** in 753 BC. At its peak, the Roman Empire covered much of Europe, North Africa and the Middle East, and it's eastern offshoot, the Byzantine Empire endured until 1453.

The Romans inspired many imitators: The **Holy Roman Empire** was founded when Charlemagne was crowned by Pope Leo III in Rome in 800, and only dissolved in 1806; the titles **Kaiser** (Germany) and **Tsar** (Russia) stem from "Caesar".

f the Western Roman Empire in 476 AD to its unifica-
a disparate collection of **city states and territories**,
which was an independent republic from 476 to
by the Medicis among others from the tenth century
Genoa – a republic from 1100 to 1805. Other cities were dom-
inated by particular families – the Sforzas and others in Milan; the Scaligeris in Verona – and the Counts of Savoy ruled in Turin from 1050 to 1860s when they became the Italian royal family.

Bologna has the oldest **university** in Europe, founded in 1060.

The term **Risorgimento** refers to the period of struggle for Italian unification in the face of foreign rule, beginning in Turin and lasting several decades, ending in 1870 with the fall of Rome and the end of papal rule in the city. Guiseppe Garibaldi (1807–1882) remains its most famous leader – the general made a wildly popular visit to England in 1864, and the Garibaldi biscuit was created in his honour.

Benito Mussolini (1883-1945) ruled Italy 1922-1945, the world's first fascist dictator. The word *fascio* was first used in the 1870s in Italy, giving way to "fascism" in the 1920s.

Cosa Nostra

The Sicilian **mafia** evolved from small bands of outlaws in the mid-nineteenth century, but became associated with organized crime in the 1920s. Their most high profile victim was magistrate Giovanni Falcone, blown up in 1992 – his replacement was killed two months later. *Capo dei capi* (the Corleonesi family boss) Bernardo Provenzano was captured in 2006. Other notable mafia groups include the **Camorra** (literally "gang") of Naples, Campania, the **Ndrangheta** of Calabria and **Sacra Corona Unita** of Brindisi, Puglia.

"I think that Dante was hip-hop culture because he wrote in vernacular Italian, and at the time that was unheard of; people wrote in Latin or Petrarch wrote in high Italian, and so Dante was talking street stuff."

Jim Jarmusch

 # Ten Italian Festas

Canelli under Attack, Canelli. June.

Corsa dei Ceri, Gubbio. May.

Festa del Redentore, Venice. July.

Festa dei Serpari, Cocullo. May.

Festival dei Due Mondi, Spoleto. July.

Giostra di Saracino, Arezzo. September.

Ivrea Carnival, Ivrea. February/March.

Il Palio, Siena. July & September.

Venice Carnival, Venice. February/March.

Viareggio Carnival, Viareggio. February/March.

 # Literature

Shakespeare, who as a young man was inspired by the Roman poet **Ovid**, set twelve plays in or around Italy. The Romantic poets loved Italy: **Goethe** and **Coleridge** travelled there, **Byron** fought for it and **Shelley** and **Keats** both died in Italy.

▶▶ Italian Literature

Italy's groundbreaking playwright **Luigi Pirandello** won the Nobel Prize in 1934, one of six Italian winners – the most recent was **Dario Fo** in 1997. Whilst not well-known overseas, the most popular Italian novel is *The Betrothed* (1842) by **Alessandro Manzoni**.

▶▶ Five Italian classics

The Adventures of Pinocchio Carlo Collodi. One of the most famous and beloved characters in children's literature.

The Betrothed Alessandro Manzoni. The great Italian nineteenth-century novel.

Decameron Giovanni Boccaccio. A collection of one hundred highly allegorical short stories.

Divine Comedy Dante Aligheri. A journey through Heaven and Hell – the greatest literary work of medieval Europe.

The Leopard Giuseppe di Lampedusa. Historical Sicilian novel recounting the tortuous nineteenth-century history of the Italian South.

▶▶ Five modern Italian classics

Confessions of Zeno Italo Svevo. This wonderful early twentieth-century comic novel has a modern self-consciousness that was way ahead of its time.

The Conformist Alberto Moravia. Psychological novel about a man dragged into the abyss of fascism.

The Garden of the Finzi-Continis Giorgio Basssani. Gentle, elegiac novel set in the Jewish community of Ferrara during the fascist period.

Invisible Cities Italo Calvino. A fictional conversation between Kublai Khan and Marco Polo.

Name of the Rose Umberto Eco. This tightly plotted monastic detective story was one of the great Italian literary successes of the modern era.

"Italy is now a great country to invest in . . . today we have fewer communists and those who are still there deny having been one. Another reason to invest in Italy is that we have beautiful secretaries . . . superb girls."

Silvio Berlusconi

 Politics

Giorgio Napolitano was elected President of Italy in May 2006 and is the country's head of state, though real power is exercised by the prime minister. Although the Italian government is notoriously unstable, with over fifty different administrations since World War II, it was effectively controlled by the same party, the Christian Democrats, until the 1990s.

"The Creator made Italy from designs by Michelangelo."

Mark Twain

Art

The Italian Renaissance is usually divided into an early period beginning in the early 1400s, and a "High" period (1480–1527), though the "proto-Renaissance" began in the twelfth-century with artists such as Nicola Pisano in Pisa and Giotto di Bondone in Padua.

▶▶ Five great works of art

The Birth of Venus Sandro Botticelli. This much-reproduced Renaissance image is now housed in the Uffizi in Florence.

Capella Brancacci, Florence. Masaccio's fifteenth-century frescoes are one of the essential sights of Florence.

Palazzo Ducale, Mantua. Mantegna's frescoes of the Gonzaga family are among the greatest treasures of the Renaissance.

The Transfiguration Raphael. Hung in its own room in the Vatican's Pinacoteca, this was thought by the French painter Poussin to be the greatest ever painting.

Basilica di San Francesco, Arrezzo. Piero della Francesca's frescoes have been recently restored to their full fifteenth-century glory.

 Holy Smoke

Italy has three active volcanos:

Mount Etna (3350m), on Sicily's east coast and the largest active volcano in Europe. Its most recent eruption was in September 2006.

Mount Vesuvius (1281m). Located just outside of Naples and most famous for the destruction of the Roman town of Pompeii in 79 AD. The last major eruption was 1944.

Stromboli (924m). One of the tiny Aeolian islands north of Sicily and in almost constant eruption; the last serious explosion was in 2003.

"Love and understand the Italians, for the people are more marvellous than the land."

E.M. Forster

 # People

The population of Italy is around 58 million. Around twelve percent of marriages end in divorce, the lowest rate in Europe. Drug addiction is the highest in Europe.

 # Top ten Italian cathedrals

Florence Known all over the world by Brunelleschi's distinctive dome.

Milan The world's largest Gothic cathedral.

Monreale Extraordinary Byzantine mosaics in this Sicilian Norman cathedral.

Orvieto Fantastically sited cathedral, dominating the countryside around it with its magnificent facade.

Parma Worth visiting for the marvellous frescoes of Correggio.

Pisa The amazing cathedral here has a lot more than the leaning tower to recommend it.

Siena Bands of black and white marble make this one of the country's most distinctive buildings.

San Giovanni in Laterano, Rome. The cathedral of Rome is not St Peter's but this, the former home of the pontiff before he moved to the Vatican.

Santa Maria dell'Assunta, Torcello, Venice. This beautiful church was Venice's first cathedral.

San Marco, Venice. Perhaps the most fascinating cathedral in Europe, with incredible thirteenth-century mosaics.

 # Coffee

Espresso was invented in Italy in 1901 when manufacturer Luigi Bezzera created the first espresso maker, though Achille Gaggia perfected the modern machine in 1938. The **cappuccino** is often assumed to have been invented in Italy, but was more likely the creation of Fred Landi, a San Francisco café owner, in 1938.

 **Gelato**

The creation of Italian *ice cream* is usually credited to Bernardo Buontalenti in sixteenth century Florence: *sorbetto* comes from Sicily.

"You may have the universe if I may have Italy."
Giuseppe Verdi

 **Opera**

Opera, meaning "works" in Italian, appeared in Italy at the end of the sixteenth century: Jacopo Peri's *Euridice* (1600) is considered the oldest opera in existence. The world's most performed operas are all Italian: Verdi's *La Traviata*, and Puccini's *La Bohème, Tosca* and *Madama Butterfly*.

The *castrati* were male sopranos, castrated before maturity. The practice was banned in Italy in 1870 – the last *castrato*, Alessandro Moreschi, died in 1922.

Bankers

Florence was the banking centre of Europe in the fourteenth century, and by 1338 there were over eighty banking houses based in the city, led by the Bardi, Peruzzi and Acciaiuoli. The Bardi and Peruzzi banks collapsed after massive defaults by King Edward III of England in 1341.

The world's oldest bank is Banca Monte dei Paschi di Siena, founded in 1472.

Romance

Giacomo Casanova (1725–1798), a Venetian, claimed to have slept with 122 women in his autobiography, and Italians are often stereotyped as the world's greatest lovers. However, the Durex Sex Survey (2005) placed Italy twentieth in terms of frequency of sex (106 times per year compared to winner Greece at 138 times).

Ultimate experiences
Italy
small print

ROUGH GUIDES – don't just travel

We hope you've been inspired by the experiences in this book. To us, they sum up what makes Italy such an extraordinary and stimulating place to travel. There are 24 other books in the 25 Ultimate Experiences series, each conceived to whet your appetite for travel and for everything the world has to offer. As well as covering the globe, the 25s series also includes books on **Journeys**, **World Food**, **Adventure Travel**, **Places to Stay**, **Ethical Travel**, **Wildlife Adventures** and **Wonders of the World**.

When you start planning your trip, Rough Guides' new-look guides, maps and phrasebooks are the ultimate companions. For 25 years we've been refining what makes a good guidebook and we now include more colour photos and more information – on average 50% more pages – than any of our competitors. Just look for the sky-blue spines.

Rough Guides don't just travel – we also believe in getting the most out of life without a passport. Since the publication of the bestselling Rough Guides to **The Internet** and **World Music**, we've brought out a wide range of lively and authoritative guides on everything from **Climate Change** to **Hip-Hop**, from **MySpace** to **Film Noir** and from **The Brain** to **The Rolling Stones**.

Publishing information

**Rough Guide 25 Ultimate experiences
Italy** Published May 2007 by Rough Guides Ltd,
80 Strand, London WC2R 0RL
345 Hudson St, 4th Floor,
New York, NY 10014, USA
14 Local Shopping Centre, Panchsheel Park,
New Delhi 110017, India
Distributed by the Penguin Group
Penguin Books Ltd,
80 Strand, London WC2R 0RL
Penguin Group (USA)
375 Hudson Street, NY 10014, USA
Penguin Group (Australia)
250 Camberwell Road, Camberwell,
Victoria 3124, Australia
Penguin Books Canada Ltd,
10 Alcorn Avenue, Toronto, Ontario,
Canada M4V 1E4
Penguin Group (NZ)
67 Apollo Drive, Mairangi Bay, Auckland 1310,
New Zealand

Printed in China
© Rough Guides 2007
80pp
A catalogue record for this book is available
from the British Library
ISBN: 978-1-84353-821-9
The publishers and authors have done
their best to ensure the accuracy
and currency of all the information in
**Rough Guide 25 Ultimate experiences
Italy**, however, they can accept no
responsibility for any loss, injury, or
inconvenience sustained by any traveller as
a result of information or advice contained
in the guide.

1   3   5   7   9   8   6   4   2

Rough Guide credits

Editors: Geoff Howard, Martin Dunford
Design & picture research: Link Hall, Jj Luck
Cartography: Maxine Repath, Katie Lloyd-Jones
Cover design: Diana Jarvis, Chloë Roberts

Production: Aimee Hampson, Katherine Owers
Proofreaders: Megan McIntyre, Nikki Birrell
Index/Next Steps: Philippa Hopkins

The authors

Jonathan Buckley (Experiences 1, 5, 9, 16, 24)
is the author of the Rough Guide to Venice,
co-author of the Rough Guides to Tuscany &
Umbria and Florence, and has also published
four novels.
James McConnachie (Experiences 2, 17) is a
contributor to the Italy and Venice guides.
Martin Dunford (Experiences 3, 6, 14, 15, 19, 21,
23) is Publishing Director of Rough Guides and
author of the Rough Guides to Rome and Italy.
Greg Witt (Experience 4) is a US-based
adventurer and travel writer.
Stephen Keeling (Experience 7, Miscellany) is
the author of the Rough Guide to Taiwan but
Italy is his favourite country.
Jeffrey Kennedy (Experiences 8, 11) is a
contributor to the Rough Guide to Italy and has
written about Italy for other publications.

Mark Ellwood (Experience 10) is a US-based
Rough Guide author who travels to – and writes
about – Italy regularly.
Ros Belford (Experience 12) lives on a remote
island off the coast of Sicily and is an author of
the Rough Guide to Italy.
Siobhan Donoghue (Experience 13) is a
designer, foodie and regular visitor to Italy.
Lucy Ratcliffe (Experience 18) is co-author of
the Rough Guide to the Italian Lakes.
Matthew Teller (Experience 20) is co-author of
the Rough Guide to the Italian Lakes.
Sarah Eno (Experience 22) is a Rough Guide
editor and enthusiastic frequent visitor to Italy.
Robert Andrews (Experience 25) is co-author of
the Rough Guide to Sicily.

Picture credits

Cover Amalfi Coast, Italy © Gavin Hellier/Jupiter Images
2 St Marks Square, Venice © Mark Thomas/Alamy
6 Siena Palio contrada flags © James McConnachie/Rough Guides
8–9 Scrovegni chapel frescoes by Giotto, Padua © Hemis/Alamy; Giotto's fresco Judas's kiss © Hemis/Alamy
10–11 Abruzzo National Park, Italy © Gillian Price/Alamy
12–13 Caracci's Farnese Palace ceiling © Robert Harding Picture Library Ltd/Alamy
14–15 Climber on a via ferrata route © Ashley Cooper/ Alamy
16–17 Florence Uffizi © PCL/Alamy; La Primavera by Botticelli © Art Kowalsky/Alamy
18–19 The Festival of San Gennaro, Naples © Adam Eastland/Alamy
20–21 The Last Supper fresco © Visual Arts Library (London)/Alamy
22–23 Capri Blue Grotto © LOOK Die Bildagentur der Fotografen GmbH/Alamy
24–25 The Palazzo Ducale, Urbino © Andre Jenny/Alamy
26–27 Parmesan Cheese © Martin Richardson/ Rough Guides; Italian Sausage Luganiga tradizionale © Martin Richardson/Rough Guides; Rows of Italian Meats and Olives © Martin Richardson/Rough Guides; Salami on counter, Bologna © Martin Richardson/Rough Guides; Hanging Salami © Martin Richardson/Rough Guides; Parma Ham © Martin Richardson/ Rough Guides
28–29 Alpine Ibex, Gran Paradiso National Park © blickwinkel/Alamy
30–31 Volcanic eruption, Stromboli © Arco Images/Alamy
32–33 Truffle hunting with a Lagotto © CuboImages srl/Alamy; White truffles from Alba Piemonte © Cephas Picture Library/Alamy
34–35 Siena Palio © James McConnachie/ Rough Guides; Siena Palio contrada flags © James McConnachie/Rough Guides
36–37 The Hall of Mysteries Pompeii © Visual Arts Library (London)/Alamy
38–39 Evening sunlight falls on San Gimignano towers, Tuscany © Cephas Picture Library/ Alamy
40–41 Detail of facade, Santa Croce church, Lecce © mcx images/Alamy; Baroque Details of Santa Croce Church Lecce © Jon Arnold Images/Alamy
42–43 Milan Shopper with Bags © PCL/Alamy; Vittorio Emanuele II shopping centre © Stock Italia/Alamy
44–45 Bull Float, Carnival Viareggio Tuscany © CuboImages srl/Alamy; Dragon Float, Carnival Viareggio Tuscany © CuboImages srl/Alamy
46–47 Polenta e uccelli © CuboImages srl/ Alamy; Bresaola © CuboImages srl/Alamy
48–49 Crucifixion of St Peter by Caravaggio © Rough Guides
50–51 Positano, Amalfi Coast © Shotfile/Alamy
52–53 Linguine alle vongole © CuboImages srl/Alamy; Tagliatelle Carbonara © Agence Images/Alamy
54–55 The traveller exposed, Balazs Kicsiny, Biennale di Venezia 2005 © Andrea Matone/ Alamy
56–57 Greek theatre Taormina Sicily © CuboImages srl/Alamy
58 Vittorio Emanuele II shopping centre © Stock Italia/Alamy

ROUGH
DES

ROUGH
GUIDES

ROUGH
GUIDES

ROUGH
GUIDES

ROUGH
GUIDES

ROUGH
GUIDES

ROUGH
GUIDES

New Zealand

Budapest

Thailand

Greece

Punk

Italy

India

Over 70 reference books and hundreds of travel
guides, maps & phrasebooks that cover the world